A Day at the Beach
Part 2

story by Jenny Alexander
illustrated by Roger Horgan

The children were making sandcastles.

"The best one will have a prize," said Mr Hopkins.

Ben made a sandcastle as tall as himself.
"I think I will win the prize," he said.

Sam made lots of little sandcastles around a big wide pool.
"I think I will win the prize," she said.

Jojo was making a long sandcastle.
Ravi said it looked like a person.

That gave Jojo an idea.
She fetched some seaweed.

Then she found two little stones for eyes, and a lolly stick for a nose. She got lots of shells.

"It's a mermaid!" said Ravi.
"I think you will win the prize."

Meanwhile, Mouse was digging a hole. "You can't win the prize with a hole!" laughed Ben.

But Mouse did not care.
"I never win prizes," he said.

Mr Hopkins walked around.
He was looking at the sandcastles.

Then he came to Mouse.
He stopped.

Mr Hopkins looked puzzled.
"Where is your sandcastle, Mouse?"
he asked.

"You can't see it because it is under the ground," said Mouse.

"It starts at this little hole ... then it has a long tunnel ... and it finishes at the big stone.

"Shall I show you what is under the stone?"

"Yes please," said Mr Hopkins.

Mouse picked up the stone.
There was a hole under it.

In the hole there was a little mouse made of sand.
"It's a mouse's sandcastle!" said Mouse.

Pip clapped his hands.
Mr Hopkins said, "This sandcastle is the best!"
He gave Mouse the prize.

Ben frowned.
Jojo and Sam frowned too.

But then they saw how happy Mouse was.
"I have never won a prize before," he said.

Ben and Jojo and Sam smiled.

"I wonder what it is!" said Mouse.